LNWR WAGONS

Supplement No. 1

Peter Ellis

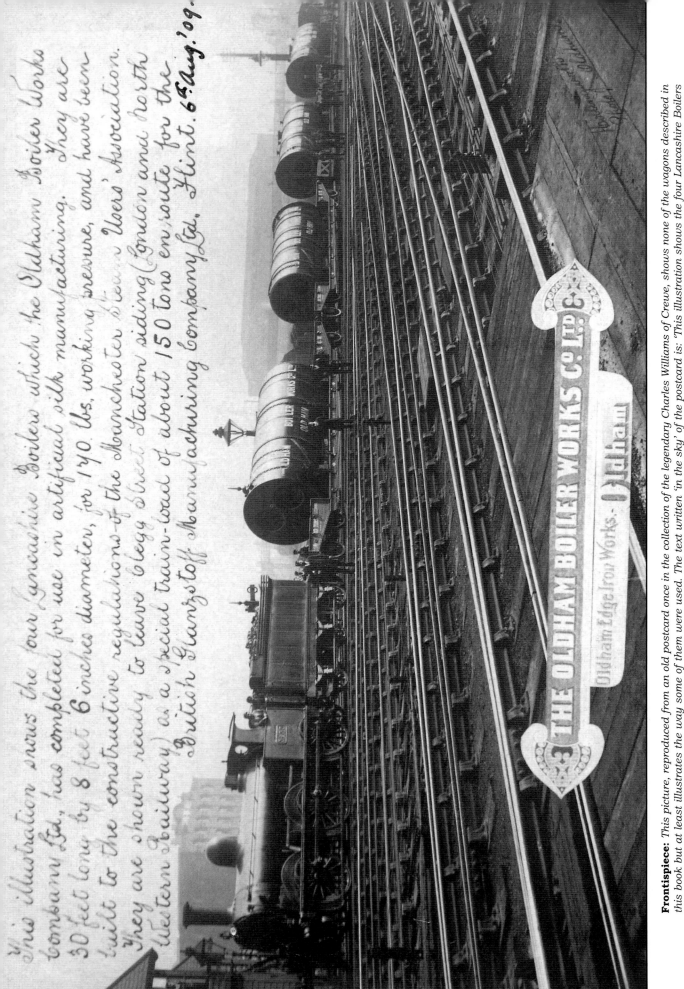

This illustration shows the four Lancashire Boilers which the Oldham Boiler Works Company Ltd. has completed for use in artificial silk manufacturing. They are 30 feet long by 8 feet 6 inches diameter, for 170 lbs. working pressure, and have been built to the constructive regulations of the Manchester Steam Users' Association. They are shown ready to leave Clegg Street Station siding (London and North Western Railway) as a special train-load of about 150 tons en route for the British Glanzstoff Manufacturing Company Ltd., Flint. 6th Aug. '09.

Frontispiece: This picture, reproduced from an old postcard once in the collection of the legendary Charles Williams of Crewe, shows none of the wagons described in this book but at least illustrates the way some of them were used. The text written 'in the sky' of the postcard is: 'This illustration shows the four Lancashire Boilers which the Oldham Boiler Works Company Ltd has completed for use in artificial silk manufacturing. They are 30ft long by 8ft 6in diameter, for 170lb working pressure, and have been built to the constructive regulations of the Manchester Steam Users' Association. They are shown ready to leave Clegg Street station siding (London & North Western Railway) in a special train load of about 150 tons en route for the British Glanzstoff Manufacturing Company Ltd, Flint.' The panel at the bottom reads: 'The Oldham Boiler Works Company Ltd, Oldham Edge Iron Works, Oldham.' The date is 6th August 1909, the engine is 'DX' class 0-6-0 No. 3427, fitted with a 2000-gallon tender, and the first two vehicles are either Diagram 101 or Diagram 102 well trolleys which were closely similar designs. If one is the former, it must be 18852 which was newly built that year in replacement of a Diagram 82 36 ton boiler trolley. Five Diagram 102 vehicles were also built in 1909 as replacements of five Diagram 78 30 ton boiler trolleys, which had become unreliable. Details of these vehicles can be found in LNWR Wagons Volume Two, chapters 4 and 5. The third vehicle is

CONTENTS

INTRODUCTION

After the London & North Western Railway was incorporated in 1846, the locomotive, carriage and wagon departments of the constituent companies continued to operate for a time as they had previously done, and it was not until the 1860s that centralisation of all activities was achieved. So far as the former Grand Junction Railway engine works at Crewe was concerned, however, the formation of the new company resulted almost immediately in greatly increased demands on its productive capacity, such that it was decided in 1847 to ease the situation by transferring the wagon works from there to Edge Hill, Liverpool. Mr Owen Owens, previously wagon foreman at Crewe, transferred with it and took charge also of the small wagon shop at Ordsall Lane, Manchester.

Despite these changes, the continuing growth of locomotive work soon restricted the space available for wagons at Edge Hill too, and the company began to search for a new site on which to centralise wagon production. In 1853 it took a £600 per year lease on Viaduct Foundry, the former engine works of Jones & Potts, just west of Newton le Willows in Lancashire, and seven years later, on 11th May 1860, it took up the option to purchase the property outright for £15,000. The factory grew progressively under the pressure to build and repair the increasing wagon stock demanded by the growing railway, and most LNWR goods wagons were built there from 1853 to 1923, when the company became part of the LMS.

By 1867 it had become clear that the work load was beyond the management capability of Mr Owens and he was replaced by Mr J. Watson Emmett, who, following in the footsteps of his father and uncle in the service of the Lancashire & Yorkshire Railway, had been appointed wagon superintendent in 1865. No doubt the move to the LNWR two years later was considered a marked career advance together with better remuneration.

Emmett remained in the post for thirty-six years and was responsible for the successful management of the works as it grew from an initial area of eight acres to over thirty-six acres by the time he retired in 1903. He was succeeded by H. D. Earl, who was in charge from 1903 to 1910. A. R. Trevithick then took over until 1916, when he was succeeded by W. W. H. Warneford, who was in charge until 1924. The works was finally closed by British Railways in the mid-1960s.

A major reference source for the study of LNWR wagons is the *Diagrams of Wagon Stock*, [National Archives, Kew, RAIL 410 1434], which was originally compiled in 1903, immediately following Emmett's retirement, and here subsequently referred to as the *1903 Diagram Book*. In its original form the book listed 82 types of wagon each nowadays colloquially referred to by its page number, for example, Diagram 47. During the next twenty years the book increased to 110 numbered pages, but as several of the earlier types were modified for particular duties, they were given their own page indicated by a suffix letter. For example, traffic coal wagons extended from their original page 64 to pages 64A, 64B, 64C and 64D with variations largely to accommodate the growing types of mechanical coaling systems. In addition to its use within the factory, copies of this book spread far and wide throughout the system to assist goods agents and others to select special wagons for whatever load they were required to transport.

There was an earlier set of wagon diagrams, which is undated but probably published in 1894 entitled *Diagrams of Trolleys and other Special Vehicles*, but few copies survive. At that time the book contained details of all the types of special wagons owned by the company. One copy, in the author's possession, must have been used within the works or drawing office, because it is heavily annotated with hand-written details of the numbers carried, the year built, the original cost, and much else besides. Consequently, it provides the earliest description of some types of wagons and is here referred to as the *1894 Diagram Book*. Those special wagons which were transferred to the LMS in 1923 were included in the *LMS Diagram Book of Specially Constructed Vehicles*, which is referred to in the text as the *LMS Diagram Book* for short.

Another documentary source is the *Table of Wagon Stock,* which is dated 30th November 1919. It lists the various types of wagons in stock by their names, and gives their carrying capacity, the number in stock, tare weights and internal dimensions, wheelbase, type of axlebox, coupling and brakes. At that time about 3000 wagons were fitted with full vacuum brakes and a further 2000 with through vacuum pipes.

The diagrams from these books are the only source of illustrations and dimensions for many of the designs. In the Historical Model Railway Society collection there are official Earlestown general arrangement drawings for only three of the eleven designs described here.

In general the diagrams and drawings available to me were in a poor state, so I have cleaned and restored them electronically, and they are now in a far better condition than they were. The size at which they are reproduced here is determined not by the need to provide a particular modelling scale, 4mm, 7mm or whatever, but to ensure that dimensions are legible and can be used by modellers in any scale.

Similarly photographs are equally scarce, if not more so, and exist for only four of the types. The collection of official Earlestown photographs in the National Railway Museum in York, referred to as 'NRM/ETN/xx', are in remarkably good condition, but the ones taken 'on the road' tend to be less clear; in this field, however, we must be thankful that any photographs survive at all.

Much use has also has been made of the *Wagon Stock Age Book*, which is preserved in the National Archives at Kew [RAIL 410 1449]. This book dates from 1902 and is stated to have been compiled from the 'Wagon Shop Registers', which unfortunately have never been found. The book tabulates each type of wagon, listing the quantities built each year and still surviving at 30th November 1902. This quantity should not be confused with the quantity originally built, as losses occurred due to accidents and general wear and tear over the years. As the annual information in the tables becomes closer to 1902, however, the more likely it becomes that it is the quantity actually built in that given year. The next volume under this title was prepared in 1909 [RAIL 410 1450], and the tables it contains were updated for each year until 1918. From this data the loss of any vehicle due to accident damage can be followed on a year-on-year basis. A third volume [RAIL 410 1451] covers the years 1919 to 1924 and so continues the sequence set up with the earlier volumes.

The wagon register number ('running' number in LMS terminology) was the number assigned to each vehicle when it was built and was carried on a cast-iron plate attached to the sole bar. It was retained by each wagon for its whole working life, and just as in the case of locomotives and carriages, when a wagon was withdrawn from service, its number was re-used on a new wagon built on revenue account 'of the type now building', as the minute book often said.

Nine of the eleven types described here were designated 'trolleys', a term used for vehicles that were longer than usual and were designed to carry exceptionally bulky or heavy loads. The later ones were usually built of riveted steel plates rather than wood, and for that reason most of them were built at Crewe rather than Earlestown because the necessary equipment and skills were to be found there.

Two volumes describing many of the types of wagons built by the company, and written by members of the London & North Western Railway Society including myself, have been published by Wild Swan Publications, *LNWR Wagons Volume One* and *Volume Two*. Excellent accounts of the painting and lettering of LNWR wagons are to be found both in *Volume One* and in *LNWR Liveries*, published by the Historical Model Railway Society in 1985.

The wagons described here are largely unusual types, some of which were only made in very small numbers . Although they did not find a place in other publications, they nevertheless are of great interest and deserve to be put on record.

Peter Ellis
Tadley
November 2011

Propeller Wagon
Diagram 47

Only one wagon of this design was produced. It was built on capital account at Earlestown in the half-year to 31st May 1884 at a cost of £90 7s 6d. It was designed for the transport of marine propellers from the manufacturers' premises to the shipyards such as those at Liverpool, Birkenhead and Barrow.

This sole example was numbered 50000 and was 24ft long over headstocks by 7ft 7in wide. No general arrangement drawing or photograph is known to survive but from the diagram in the *1903 Diagram Book*, Figure 1, it is clear that the superstructure was most unusual in that, rather than having a normal planked side, it had two large timber baulks, measuring 2ft 2in high by 2ft 3in wide, which ran along each side. The ends were open and at the centre of each baulk was a clamp into which the propeller shaft could be secured. The jaws of the clamp were adjustable to accommodate varying shaft diameters. The floor had a shallow well 17ft 6in long by 3ft 6in wide, which could possibly have been open to the rails at the bottom, because both diagrams, 1894 and 1903, quote a dimension from rail level to the bottom of the shaft clamp of 6ft 9in. This dimension would only be relevant to the design if the lower blade of the propeller could protrude below the level of the floor of the well and would ensure that the propeller remained safely clear of the rail level at all times. On this assumption, the trolley could transport propellers up to approximately 12ft in diameter comfortably within the height between the rail level and the top of the loading gauge.

It is instructive to compare this vehicle with the contemporary 24ft long timber wagon, Diagram 14, as illustrated on page 158 of *LNWR Wagons, Volume One*. The wheelbase of the propeller wagon was reduced from 16ft on the timber wagon to 14ft, and the tare weight was increased to 8 tons 12cwt 1qr, no doubt due to the heavy timber side-baulks.

The solebar and buffer beams appear to have been of standard LNWR construction, perhaps 12in deep and 5in thick. The buffer springs must have been located at each end of the frame because the central well precluded the use of central springs. The buffers were the round base 3-bolt type, which were standard at the time and consistent with the details shown in the diagram. As built, no brake is shown in the *1894 Diagram Book*, but a hand-written note has been added that a single brake was fitted to one side only. So possibly it was not fitted initially but added later. No details of the brake mechanism are shown in the diagram but it is reasonable to assert that it resembled the brake on the Diagram 14 timber wagon.

After a working life of thirty years, No. 50000 was withdrawn in 1914 and replaced with the Diagram 108 bogie well trolley, which carried the same number and largely filled the same purpose though it appears to have had a more flexible capability than the original vehicle (*LNWR Wagons Volume Two* page 191).

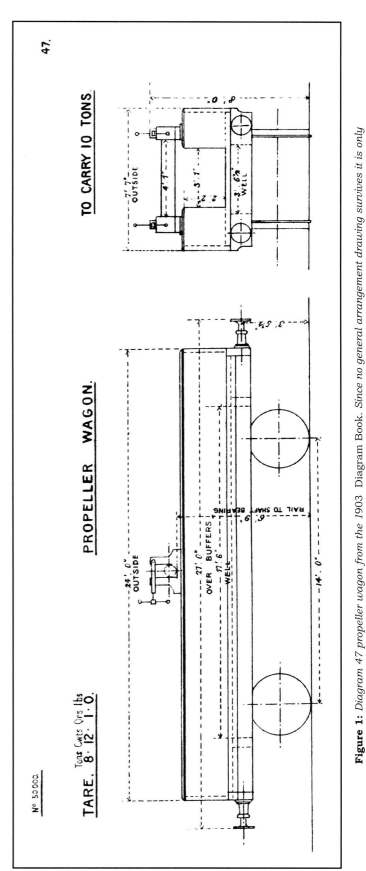

Figure 1: *Diagram 47 propeller wagon from the 1903 Diagram Book. Since no general arrangement drawing survives it is only this diagram and a near identical one from the 1894 Diagram Book that provide some of the dimensions and design details.*

Shunting Wagon Diagram 51

The first mention of shunting wagons is in Locomotive and Engineering Committee Minute 16460, 3rd August 1897, which records that two shunting wagons were to be built for the Birkenhead Extension lines, as part of a joint agreement with the GWR, which would also provide two brake vans. These two LNWR wagons were numbered 65612 and 65613 and appear on page 51 of the *1903 Diagram Book*. It is believed that this initiative was in response to Board of Trade legislation requiring all shunting operations within sidings and yards to be under the control of a 'brake van', following numerous accidents to railway staff. The LNWR saw the shunting wagon as a cheaper way to meet these requirements than the use of normal goods brake vans.

Full details of their construction are to be found in Earlestown general arrangement drawing No.34 [HMRS 1121], Figure 3-5, which is dated 5th May 1897. The body is 15ft 6in long by 7ft 3in wide, which is 5in narrower than the Diagram 1 single-plank open wagon, but with a shorter wheelbase, which is either 8ft 6in (*1903 Diagram Book*) or 8ft 9in (general arrangement drawing). The brake mechanism is similar to that fitted to the Diagram 16 10ton brake van which would account for the 8ft 6in wheelbase. The mechanism is the same even down to the cruciform support at the centre of each solebar on Diagram 16. The horizontal brake wheel operates vertically through the floor in the style of a goods brake van, and side rails provide a safe enclosure for the brakeman. The tare weight, 9 tons 4cwt, is surprisingly heavy for an open wagon but is accounted for by a boarded area beneath the floor, which was doubtless filled with scrap-iron ballast, similar to that in conventional brake vans.

No further wagons were added to the original two listed on this diagram, 65612 and 65613. Under the title of 'Shunting Wagons', however, the *1919 Table of Wagons* lists a stock of 101 vehicles and also quotes their tare weights as 9 tons 4cwt and 4 tons 4cwt 2qr. The latter is the recorded tare weight of a Diagram 1 open wagon, suggesting that 'shunting wagons' or runner wagons were created by conversion of open wagons. In support of this suggestion, Goods Conference Minute 18918, January 1900, reads: 'four low-sided wagons are to be fitted with steps etc for use as shunting wagons. Two for use at Coventry and two more for Nuneaton'.

Clearly, these vehicles were not the same as the Diagram 51 design but since there is no other diagram for them they will be described here because they were used for a similar purpose. Other minutes dated between 1902 and 1904 mention the use of converted low-sided goods wagons for use as 'shunt wagons *in lieu* of brake vans'. The allocations given in these minutes show either the quantity of wagons at each location or the numbers of the wagons concerned. These details are summarised in the tables which follow.

Shunting Wagons

Number	Location	Number	Location
1179	Crewe	10942	Garston Dock
21019	Carnforth	26889	Carnforth
65612	Birkenhead EL	7711	Birkenhead
11757	Bletchley	21373	Carnforth
28412	Birkenhead	65613	Birkenhead EL
7779	Carnforth	12006	Garston Docks.
24206	Mold Junction.	36154	Birkenhead
73843	St Helens	7960	Stafford
16447	Widnes	24299	Crewe
36158	Birkenhead	73921	Birkenhead
11035	Stafford	18477	St Helens
26569	Garston Dock	41227	Northampton
74112	Willesden		

Quantity	Location	Quantity	Location
7	Garston	2	Bickershaw
7	St. Helens	2	Coleham
5	Basford Sidings	2	Coventry
5	Widnes	2	Pemberton
2	Nuneaton	1	Whitehaven
1	Hadley Jct.	1	Albion
1	Swansea	1	Carnforth
1	Hawkesbury Lane	1	Mold Jct.

These sources account for about half of the 101 shunting wagons, which existed in 1919. Unusually, the 1919 table does not give the range of dimensions of the 101 shunting wagons it lists, so it is possible that they varied in size, perhaps widely. All were fitted with 6in by 3in journals running in grease axle boxes and had 3-link couplings. Sixty-six were fitted with brakes on both sides, while even at this late date thirty-three had brakes on one side only. Just two were fitted with screw brakes – presumably the two Birkenhead vehicles listed on the diagram. One must have been fitted for some special duty because it had a vacuum brake through pipe.

The 1923 photograph of No 29747 in Plate 5 provides the best information on how the Diagram 1 wagon was converted for runner wagon duties.

Photographs show that runner wagons were normally attached next to the shunting engine, which made operations safer and quicker by allowing shunters to ride around yards and sidings with the engine, carrying their tools on the wagon rather than having to walk between jobs, but whether they provided any brake power during these operations is unclear.

How long these shunting wagons continued in use during LMS days is not known, nor is there any evidence that the LMS built any shunting wagons to replace aging pre-grouping vehicles. But since many Midland and Great Western shunting wagons are known to have continued in use throughout the Grouping period it is reasonable to expect that some of the ex-LNWR ones survived too.

Plate 1: *Shunting/Runner wagon, converted from Diagram 1 16ft single plank open wagon, No 29747, in service as a runner wagon at Earlestown yard in 1923. The 'lift date' painted on the left end of the solebar reads '7.6.23'.*

J. P. Richards, HMRS AAH025

Plate 2: *Class 'A' three-cylinder compound 0-8-0 No. 1824 shunting at Carnforth. The engine appears to be in regular use for shunting, as it has a shunter's pole lying on the bufferbeam, three-link coupling on the front, easier for shunters to use than the screw type normnally carried there, and a shunter's truck behind the tender. It is one of those believed to have been converted from a Diagram 1 open wagon and the sun-hatted shunters standing on its footboards doubtless much prefer to ride on it than to have to walk about the yard to every wagon that requires shunting. Why the engine has two lamp sockets on the right-hand end of the bufferbeam is unknown but possibly connected with shunting at night. The date has to be after 1st February 1903 as the engine has a centre lamp socket.*

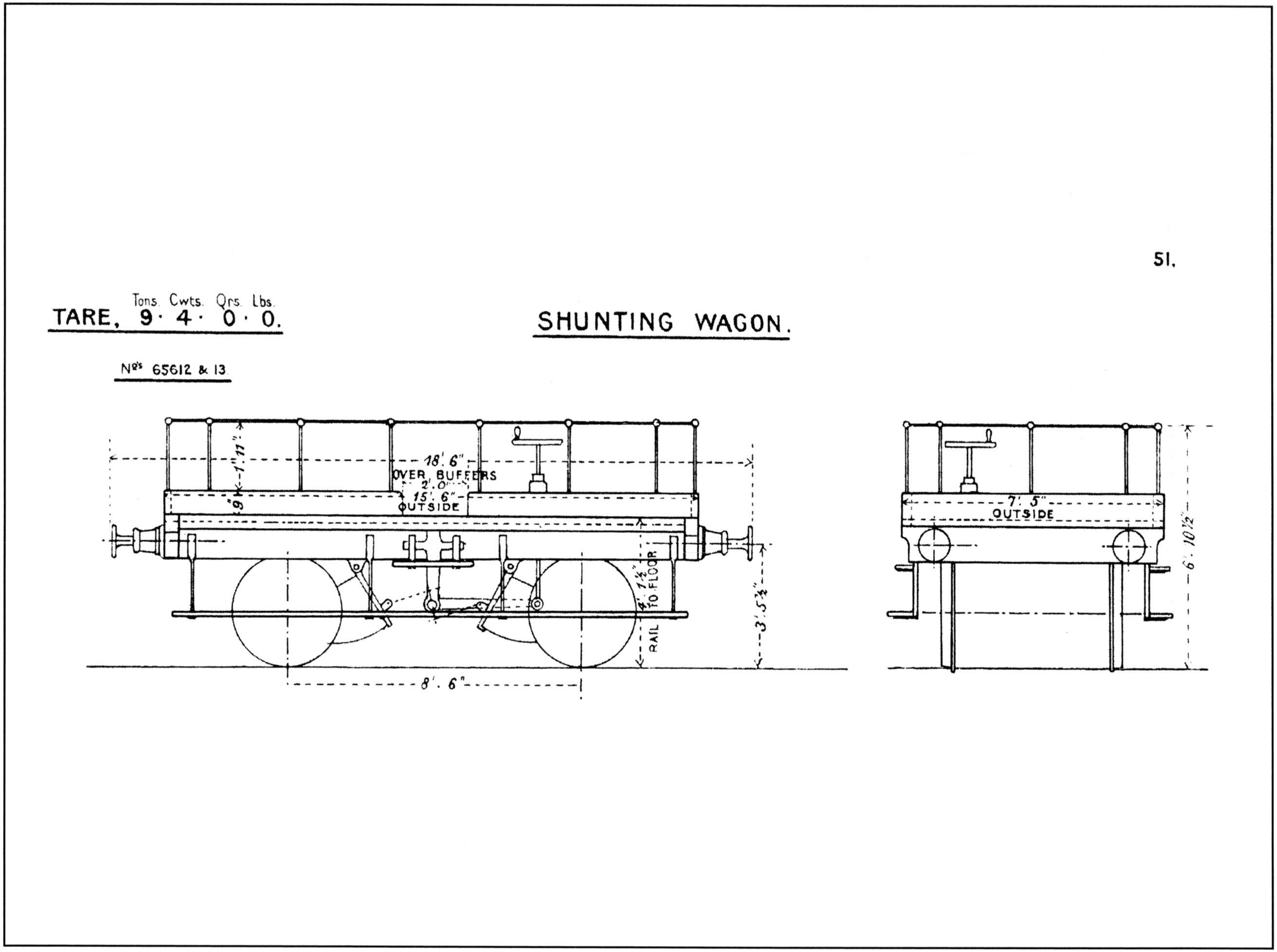

Figure 2: *Diagram 51 shunting wagon from the 1903 Diagram Book representing the two wagons which were built for the Birkenhead extension line in 1897. A comparison with the general arrangement drawing, Figure 5, shows the stanchions and railings in different positions.*

6

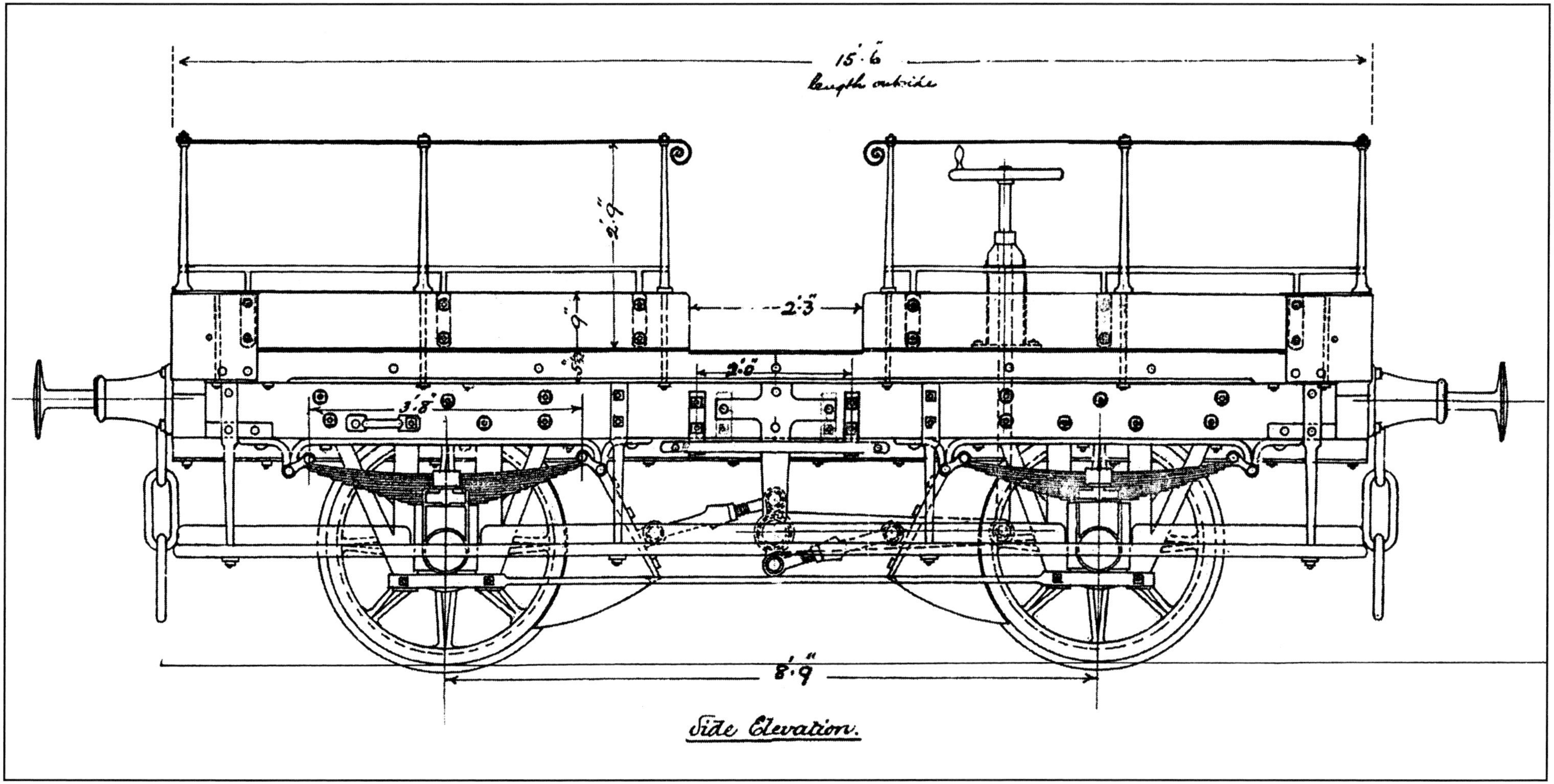

Figure 3: *Side elevation of a Diagram 51 shunting wagon from the Earlestown general arrangement drawing.* HMRS 1121

7

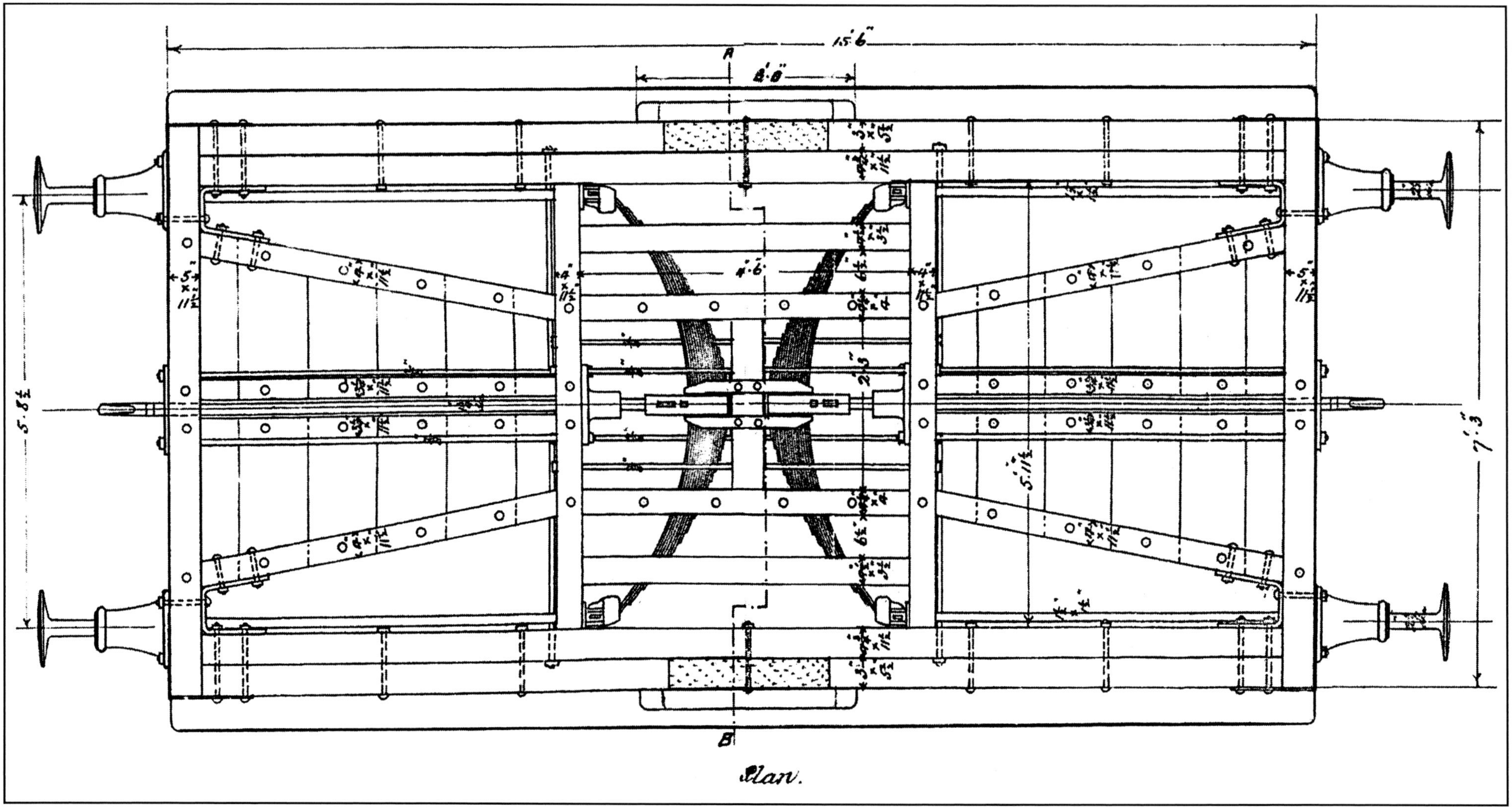

Figure 4: *Plan view of a Diagram 51 shunting wagon from the Earlestown general arrangement drawing.* HMRS 1121

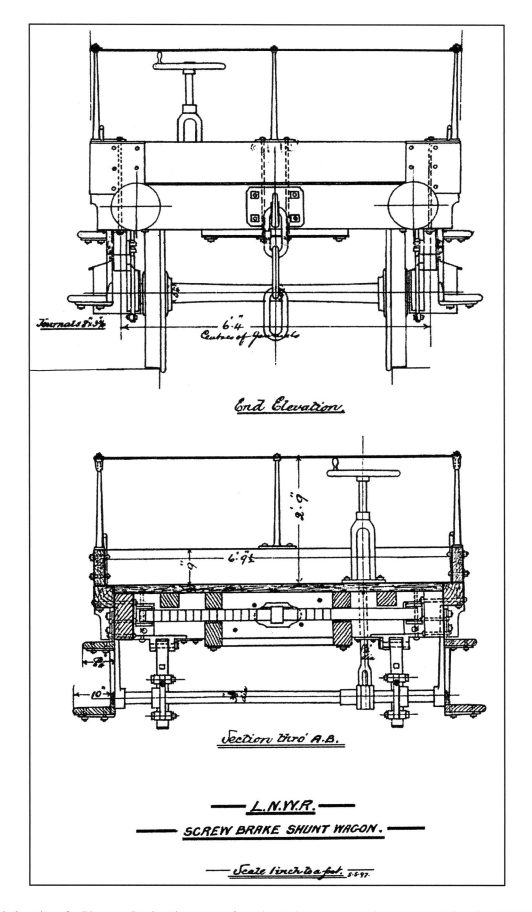

End Elevation.

Journals 8·5¼

6'·4"
Centres of Journals

2'·9"

6'·9½"

10"

Section thro' A.B.

L.N.W.R.

SCREW BRAKE SHUNT WAGON.

Scale 1 inch to a foot. 5·5·97.

Figure 5: *End elevation of a Diagram 51 shunting wagon from the Earlestown general arrangement drawing. HMRS 1121*

Agricultural Engine Trolley Diagram 67

The LNWR had two designs of agricultural engine trolley. The first, Diagram 67, was designed to carry 10 tons, and consisted of two four-wheeled vehicles built in the half year to November 1884, Nos 49993 and 49994, at a cost of £104 9s. 8d each. No photographs of these vehicles have been found, and the best representation of the design comes from the diagram on page 67 of the *1903 Diagram Book*. An Earlestown general arrangement drawing exists, but it is in poor condition, both too grubby and too distorted to reproduce more than the two detail sections shown below.

The vehicles were 25ft 6in long over headstocks with an outside width of 8ft 6in and a pair of 2ft 8in diameter wheels at each end set to a 20ft wheelbase. They were clearly capable of being end-loaded with a traction engine or similar agricultural machinery over the headstocks, which were 3ft 9½in above rail level. The load could then be lowered down a slope about 4ft long to rest on the 15ft 4in long floor of the well of the wagon which was only 2ft 8in above rail level, that is, 1ft 1½in below the headstock level. The detail from the general arrangement drawing shows how the 3ft 7in long springs and 10ton axleboxes, with 6¾in by 4in journals, were mounted on the solebars.

The drawing shows the construction of the lever-operated brake mechanism. The original drawing is heavily marked and torn, so that the copied image is distorted. These imperfections have been removed in the computer so as to render the drawing usable but much of the fine detail has been lost in the process. The single brake operated on one side only according to a note in the *1894 Diagram Book*, but was later duplicated on the other end.

Both vehicles remained in revenue service until 1914 when No. 49994 was scrapped and replaced by a 20 ton Diagram 78 vehicle of similar appearance, as described below. The other one, No. 49993, entered LMS service in 1923 and is shown on page 42 of the *LMS Diagram Book* as a 10 ton implement truck [code IPH]. One copy of this book is annotated with the information that it was 'broken up on 14.9.1936'. The LMS diagram, unusually, does not have a plan view, but the notes reveal that it had an all-wood floor. It was fitted with a lever brake at each end and could negotiate a curve of 2 chains. The tare weight had been increased to 7tons 4cwt perhaps due in part to the extra brake mechanism, and the load was secured to the vehicle by four sets of binding chains.

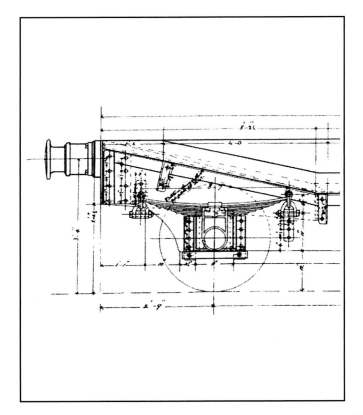

Figure 6: *End detail of Diagram 67 trolley.*

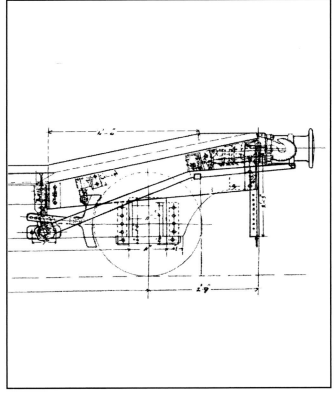

Figure 7: *Brake detail of Diagram 67 trolley.*

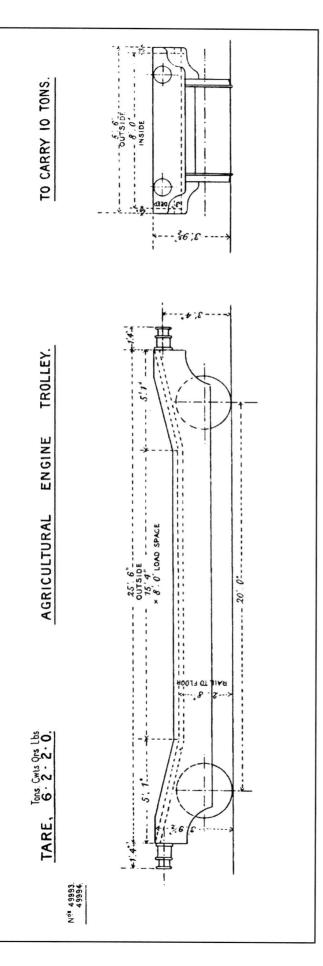

Figure 8: *Diagram 67 agricultural engine trolley from the 1903 Diagram Book.*

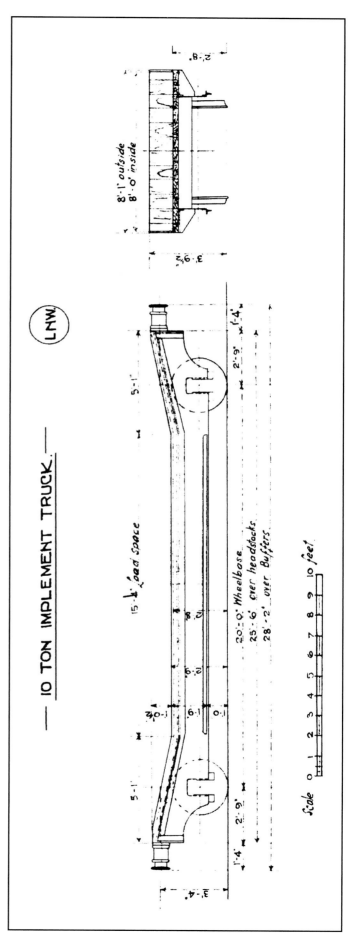

Figure 9: *Diagram from page 42 of the LMS Diagram Book, where it is described not as an 'agricultural engine trolley' but merely as a 10 ton 'implement truck'.*

Plae 3: *Class 'G1' 0-8-0 No. 326, built in 1913, approaching Northampton on 22nd May 1921 with an out-of-gauge special conveying rotary kilns from Barrow in Furness to Poplar. The first vehicle behind the engine is a Diagram 17A brake van but then comes a Diagram 105 trolley. The next wagon seems not to be LNWR and then the angle becomes too acute to identify subsequent vehicles.*
Leslie J. Thompson

Agricultural Engine Trolley Diagram 78

The 20 ton version of the agricultural engine trolley, built presumably to cope with the increasing size and weight of traction engines and so forth, appeared in 1910. It was put on page 78 of the *1903 Diagram Book* in place of five boiler trolleys which had resided there until they were scrapped in 1909 [*LNWR Wagons Volume Two*, page 153]. The new vehicles did not carry the numbers of the withdrawn boiler trolleys but rather the first was given the number 32911 because it was regarded as a revenue replacement for a withdrawn Diagram 68 tramcar trolley. From the diagram it can be seen that the new 20 ton trolley was 26ft 6in over headstocks and 8ft 6in wide over the bed. The wheelbase was increased to 21ft and although the diagrams do not specify the wheels used, they are likely to have been 3ft 1½in diameter with solid spokes in order to carry the load. The headstocks were 3ft 10in above

rail level. Most of the other features were similar to the earlier 10 ton design, but the flat load space was reduced to 15ft. A right-handed brake was fitted to each end and the vehicle was noted as capable of negotiating a 2-chain radius curve.

When in 1914 one of the 10 ton trollies was scrapped, possibly due to an accident, it was replaced with a second 20 ton vehicle, No. 49994. Both were inherited by the LMS in 1923 and were placed on page 54 of the *LMS Diagram Book*. One copy of this book records that eventually, at some time in the 1950's, one of these vehicles was 'transferred to the service stock' and the other was 'broken up'. The *BR Withdrawal Register* records that 249994 was scrapped in 1956, but makes no mention of 232911. However, it is believed from a photograph that it was indeed 232911 which outlasted its partner, 249994.

12

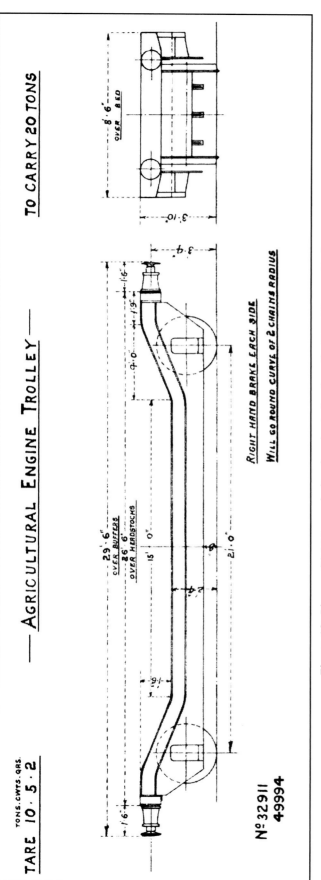

Figure 10: *Diagram 78 20 ton agricultural engine trolley from the 1903 Diagram Book.*

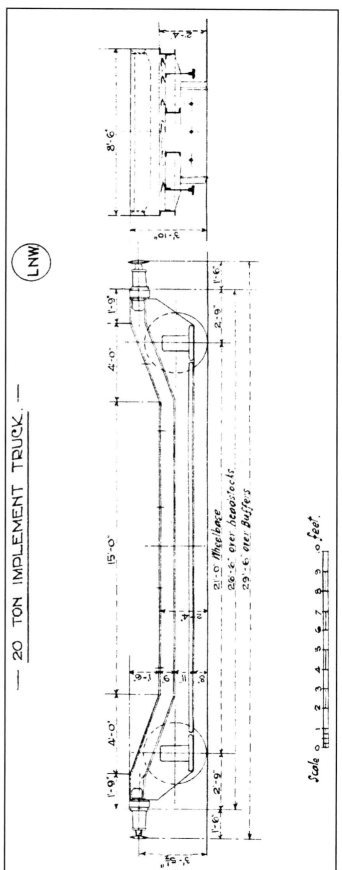

Figure 11: *Diagram from page 54 of the LMS Diagram Book, where it is described not as an 'agricultural engine trolley' but merely as a 20 ton 'implement truck'.*

13

Dock Trolley to carry 25 tons
Diagram 73

The only details available of this trolley are from 1894 *Diagram Book,* where it is described as a 'Dock Trolley to carry 25 tons', and from the *1903 Diagram Book,* where it is simply a 'Trolley to carry 20 tons'. Neither book gives the date of construction but from its number, 22052, it seems to have been built about 1865.

From a note on the 1894 diagram the trolley was rated to carry 25 tons but did not run on the main line; rather it was used exclusively at Liverpool Dock Goods station for 'Dock Traffic' and was lettered 'Waterloo Station, Dock Rails'. In the *1903 Diagram Book* it was 18ft 4in over its dumb buffers, 15ft 6in over headstocks with an outside width of 6ft 9½in. From its general shape it seems to have been of wooden construction and with the familiar 8ft 6in wheelbase. The brakes blocks look similar to those of the Diagram 16 brake van and the diagram shows them operating on both wheels on one side only by means of an approximately 14-inch diameter hand wheel located close to the centre of the solebar. The removable bolsters were 12in by 13½in and were shaped to accommodate a cylindrical vessel of up to 8 ft in diameter. The centre of the bolster was 4ft 6in above rail level. The tare weight was 5 tons 3cwt 2qr when fitted with the bolsters and 4 tons 14cwt 2qr without.

A note on some copies of the 1894 diagram states that 'the trolley was repaired, painted and the bolsters removed in March 1903' before being sent into ordinary traffic lettered 'To carry 20 tons'. This renovation was just in time to warrant giving the vehicle its own page in the *Diagram Book,* but the change seems to have been unsuccessful, because the trolley was scrapped only four years later in 1907, its number being transferred to a Diagram 97 40 ton platform trolley [*LNWR Wagons Volume Two*, page 172].

Platform Trolley to carry 20 tons
Diagram 74

Ten of the 20ton Diagram 74 platform trolleys were built progressively on renewal account between the half-year to November 1869 and the half-year to November 1882. The detail is listed in the table below which is reproduced from a heavily annotated copy of the *1894 Diagram Book.*

No.	Date built	Cost			Account	Wheels
		£	S	d		
18859	Nov 1881	46	14	4	Renewal	old
18860	May 1874	44	2	8	"	old
20247	May 1870	44	2	8	"	new
20265	Nov 1869	86	0	8	"	new
20289	May 1870	86	8	11	"	new
20296	Nov 1882	47	11	4	"	old
20338	May 1870	86	8	11	"	new
20359	May 1870	86	8	11	"	new
22050	May 1880	44	10	1	"	old
22051	May 1876	62	10	9	"	old

No general arrangement drawing has been found, but two diagrams show the main features. The body was 24ft long over headstocks with an outside width of 7ft 10in. Built largely of wood, it was similar to the 24ft long Diagram 14 timber wagon, but there was a short slope, 2ft 9in long, at each end, leading from the headstock level to a planked load space four inches lower than the top of the curb rail and with a level surface 18ft 6in long. The buffers were self-contained with the rather low centre height of 3ft 2½in, but no details are shown of the wheels, axleguards or axleboxes. The six wheels were set on 9ft centres and a hand brake was fitted to one wheel on one side only. There were some dimensional variations, due probably to the long period over which they were built. For example, 20296 measured only 7ft 4in wide inside and 22050 was only 22ft long but 8ft 8in wide with a completely flat top – that is, it had no sides or ends. It had a wheelbase of 7ft 7in + 7ft 7in, rather than the 9ft + 9ft of all the others.

All ten remained in revenue service until 1907, when they were progressively replaced with new trollies as part of a general upgrade at that time because of the poor condition of most of the company's early trollies. No.20338 was authorised to be broken up in Goods Conference minute 20928 of 15th May 1907 and was replaced with a 40 ton Diagram 97 trolley [*LNWR Wagons Volume Two*, page 172]. The following year Nos. 18859, 20247, 20265, 20289 and 22050 were also replaced with Diagram 97 trollies. In 1910 No. 22051 was withdrawn and replaced with the unique Diagram 104 ingot trolley [see page 19]. In 1911 No. 20296 was scrapped and replaced by a Diagram 107 timber trolley [*LNWR Wagons Volume One,* page 165], while No. 20359 was reused on a Diagram 100 40 ton trolley [*LNWR Wagons Volume Two,* page 179], and finally in 1917 No.18860 was replaced with a Diagram 105 well trolley.

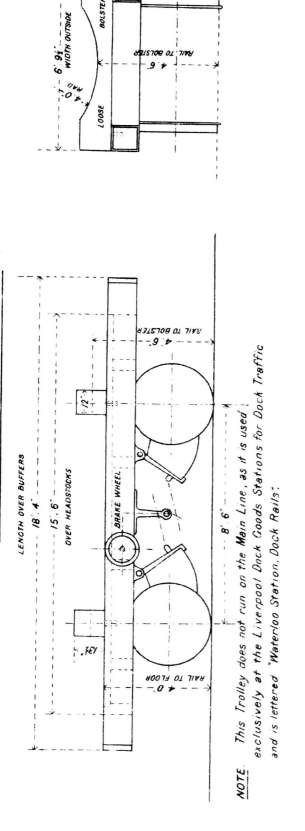

DOCK TROLLEY (25 TONS). № 22052.

LENGTH OVER BUFFERS

18'·4"

15'·6"

OVER HEADSTOCKS

BRAKE WHEEL

RAIL TO BOLSTER
4'·6"

8'·6"

12"

13½"

RAIL TO FLOOR
4'·0"

WIDTH OUTSIDE
16'·9"·7'

RAD
4'·0"

BOLSTERS

RAIL TO BOLSTER
4'·6"

LOOSE

NOTE: This Trolley does not run on the Main Line, as it is used exclusively at the Liverpool Dock Goods Stations for Dock Traffic and is lettered "Waterloo Station, Dock Rails".

15

Figure 12, above: *Diagram of the 25 ton dock trolley from the 1894 Diagram Book.*

Figure 13, below: *Diagram of platform trolley from the 1903 Diagram Book.*

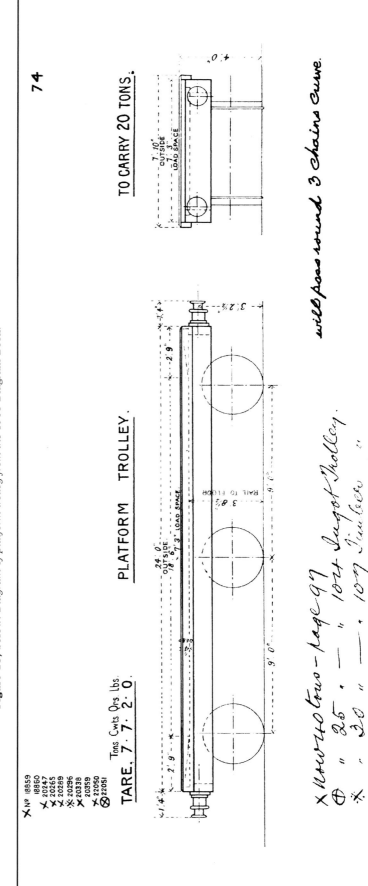

74

TO CARRY 20 TONS.

7'·10"
OUTSIDE
7'·3"
LOAD SPACE

4'·0"

PLATFORM TROLLEY.

24'·0"
OUTSIDE
18'·6"
7'·3" LOAD SPACE

3'·8½" RAIL TO FLOOR

9'·0"

9'·6"

2'·9"

4'¼"

3'·2½"

2'·9"·4"

7'·4"

X N° 18859
18860
X 20247
X 20265
X 20289
※ 20296
X 20338
20359
X 22050
⊗ 22051

Tons Cwts Qrs. lbs.
TARE. 7· 7· 2· 0.

X *Now 40 tons — page 97*
⊕ " 25 " — " 1074 Sugar Trolley.
X " 30 " — " 1079 Timber "

will pass round 3 chains Curve.

Platform Trolley to carry 30 tons
Diagram 80

A 30 ton platform trolley, Diagram 80, was also introduced at about the same time as the 20 ton Diagram 74. Two vehicles, Nos. 39851 and 39852, were built to this design on the capital account in the half year to May 1875. They were two feet shorter than the 20 ton trolleys and the wheelbase was reduced to 7ft 4in + 7ft 4in. The floor was completely flat, so despite the shorter overall length, the available load space, at 21ft 7in, was three feet longer than the Diagram 74 equivalents.

They remained in service for over thirty years until, in 1908, No. 39852 was scrapped, its number being re-used by a Diagram 97 40 ton platform trolley, [*LNWR Wagons Volume Two*, page 172] as were those of the six Diagram 74 vehicles. A year later in 1909, No. 39851 was also withdrawn and its number re-used for the first of the newly built glass trolleys to Diagram 99 [*LNWR Wagons Volume One*, page 181].

Wire Rope Trolley Diagram 98

The wire rope trolley was built to transport wire ropes between Crewe and the tunnels at Liverpool, namely those between Edge Hill and Lime Street passenger station and between Edge Hill and Wapping and Waterloo Goods stations. Rope haulage was replaced by locomotives in Lime Street tunnel in March 1870 and in Wapping Tunnel on 11th May 1896. Waterloo tunnel was operated by locomotives as far as Byrom Street and thence by endless steel rope via the Victoria Tunnel to Edge Hill. The rope broke on 16th February 1895 and after that traffic was worked by locomotives. Vehicles were pulled up the gradients and allowed to run down them by gravity. Wire ropes were also used on the Cromford & High Peak section, so it seems probable that the wire rope trolley was used to deliver ropes there also.

While employed on these duties the wire rope trolley was part of the service stock and not numbered in the general wagon list. Perhaps it saw little use when rope haulage at Liverpool ceased, but in 1907 it was refurbished to transport wire ropes from Warrington Wire Works to the company's customers around the country. Mr Whale then agreed that it should be taken into the goods stock and numbered 72426 (Goods Traffic Committee minute 8253, dated 18th December 1907). Presumably, as chief mechanical engineer responsible

for Crewe Works, where the wire ropes had been manufactured, the wire rope trolley was part of his service stock.

No general arrangement drawing is known, and as it was a 'one-off', its consruction cannot be deduced from similar wagons. The only details of its shape and size come from the diagram on page 98 of the *1903 Diagram Book*. The drums, which carried the rope, were 11ft 1in in diameter and approximately 6ft wide. They were supported on either side by wrought-iron girders 28ft long. These longitudinal girders were linked by cross girders at either end which in turn mated with the central pivots on the four-wheeled bogies on which the whole vehicle ran. The bogies had a wheel base of 8ft 3in and the wheels were remarkably large at 3ft 11in in diameter. A vertical screw handle operated the brakes on each bogie, but there is no evidence as to the design and construction of the brake mechanism. The distance between bogie centres was only 24ft 6in which is shorter than many of the company's bogie trolleys and made it more manoeuvrable than most. Certainly there were no limitations written on the sketch as to the minimum curve it could negotiate.

It continued in service until 1922 when it was scrapped, its number being re-used by one of the final two Diagram 100 40ton trolleys.

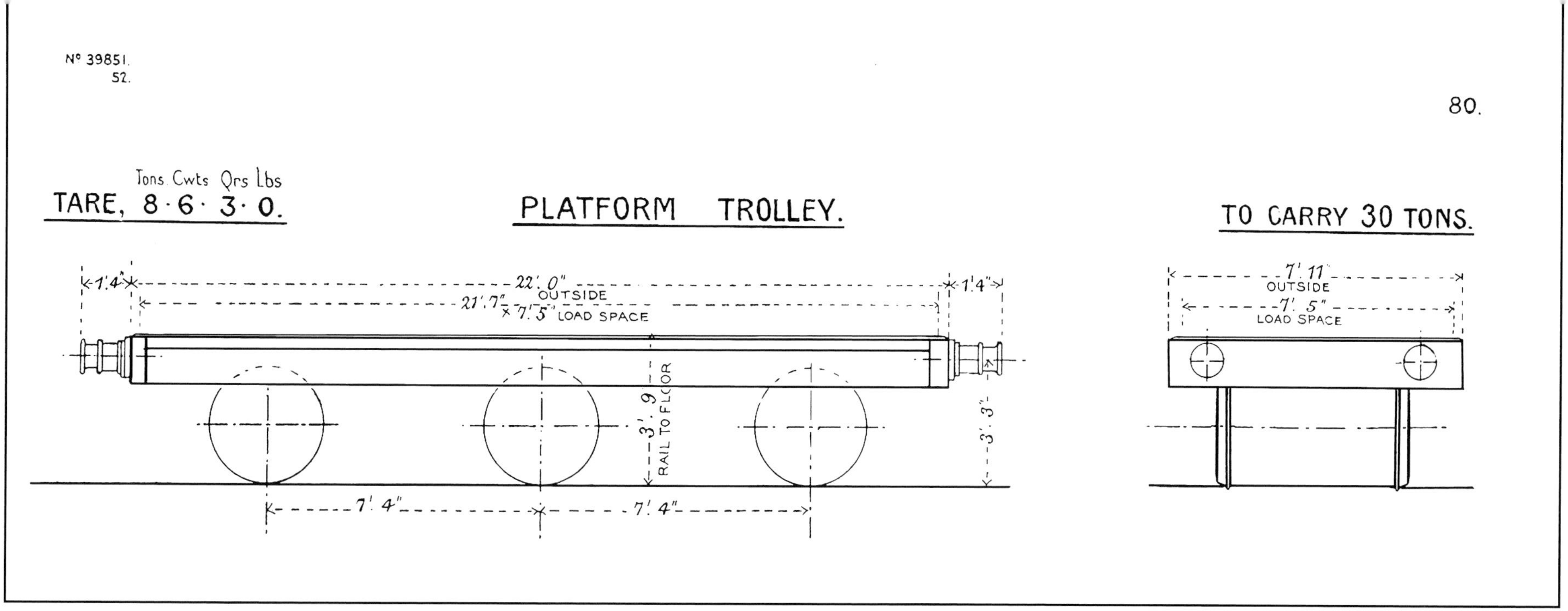

Figure 14: *Diagram of the 30 ton six-wheeled platform trolley to Diagram 80 from the 1903 Diagram Book.*

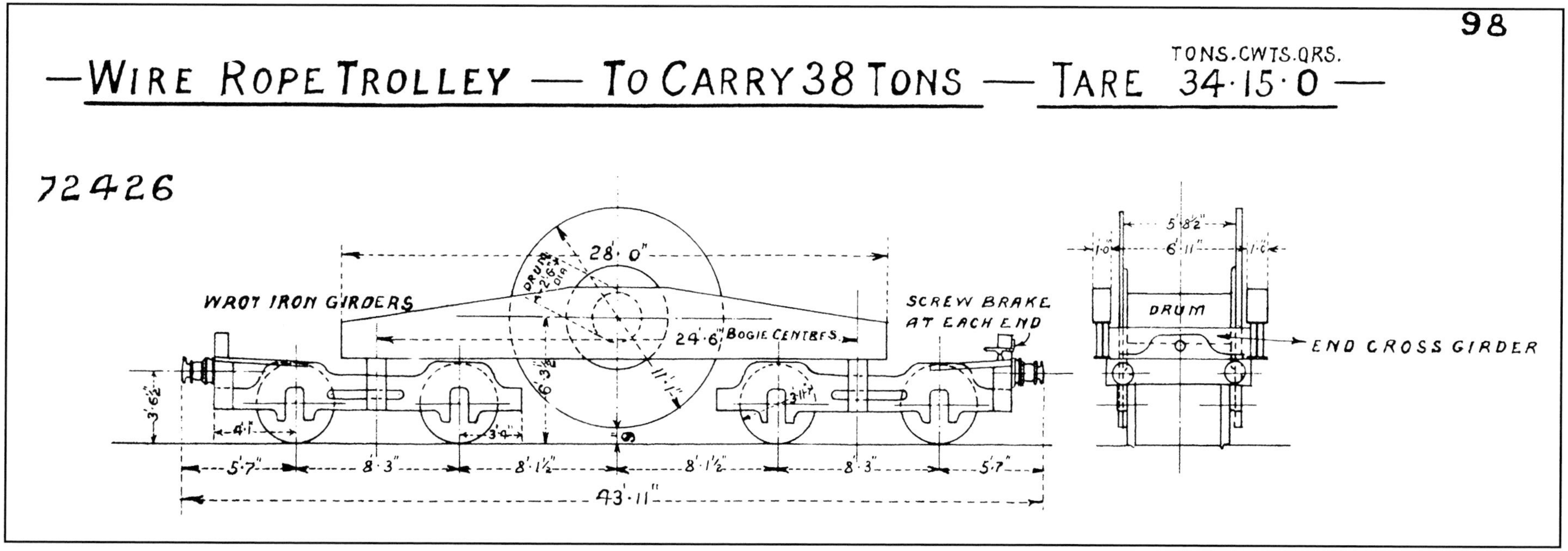

Figure 15: *This is the only known illustration of the wire rope trolley and is Diagram 98 in the 1903 Diagram Book.*

Ingot Trolley to carry 25 tons
Diagram 104

Ingot Trolley No. 22051 to Diagram 104 was a unique vehicle. Goods Traffic Committee Minute 21712, dated 14th February 1910, recommended that condemned Diagram 74 trolley No. 22051 should be replaced with a 25 ton 'Trolley with Stanchions' at a cost of £120, especially for use at Messers Bessemer's Steel Works in Bolton. The recommendation was authorised by a subsequent board meeting, and the vehicle was built in the half year to May 1910. It appears on page 104 of the *1903 Diagram Book*. In addition to carrying steel ingots it was reported also to be suitable for the carriage of engine beds, armatures and locomotive frames. It was able to negotiate curves of as small as one chain radius, which was probably an original requirement because Bessemer's track layout had some very tight curves, and the short wheelbase, 9ft 6in long, enabled it to use the numerous 10ft wagon turntables in Bessemer's plant.

The body was 16ft long over headstocks and had an outside width of 7ft 8in. The frame was constructed from four longitudinal channel-section girders, as shown in the cross-section diagram in the *LMS Diagram Book*. The rivet heads visible on the solebar in the official photograph indicate that the solebars are linked together by cross members riveted at right angles with angle brackets. The floor was constructed of stout oak planks 10in by 3in bolted to the top of the girder frame. The shackles were so large that, unlike on most other trolleys, they did not nestle within the solebar channel but were located along the solebar, as seen in the photograph and in the LMS diagram. The five stanchions were aligned along the outer edge of each side, each stanchion fitting into a socket, possibly steel-lined, in the 3in thick oak floor, and were spaced as in the LNWR diagram. Whether there were alternative locations is not known. The photograph is the only source of information on the brake gear, which was lever-operated on both wheels on each side of the vehicle.

The trolley was fitted with 10-spoke wheels supported on 11in by 6in journals running in square, flat-fronted axle boxes [*LNWR Wagons Volume One*, page 43). The buffers were the longer type, 13in body casting, with four-bolt attachment (*LNWR Wagons Volume One*, page 52) and the buffer heads were oval. A tie bar was fitted between the axle guards to prevent them splaying outwards under load. The couplings were the three-link pattern with a long middle link to allow for the longer buffers.

The original LNWR livery is shown in the photograph, but because the curb rail is so narrow there is space for only very small diamonds. The vehicle passed to the LMS in 1923 and appears on page 37 of the *LMS Diagram Book*, where it is described as a 'flat truck' (code F.R.) and is shown without stanchions, probably due to a change of use because Bessemer's Steel Works had closed down in 1924. There is no knowledge of the LMS livery but it is reasonable to assume that it was similar, with the letters 'LMS' and the new number plates replacing the originals at the same locations. The vehicle worked right through the LMS period and passed to BR in 1948, but was withdrawn shortly afterwards in 1949.

Plate 4: *Official photograph of 22051 on completion in June 1910. The details of the stanchions and binding chains are useful, since no general arrangement drawing is known. The shackles are too large to fit within the U-shaped girder that forms the solebar.*

NRM/ETN 81

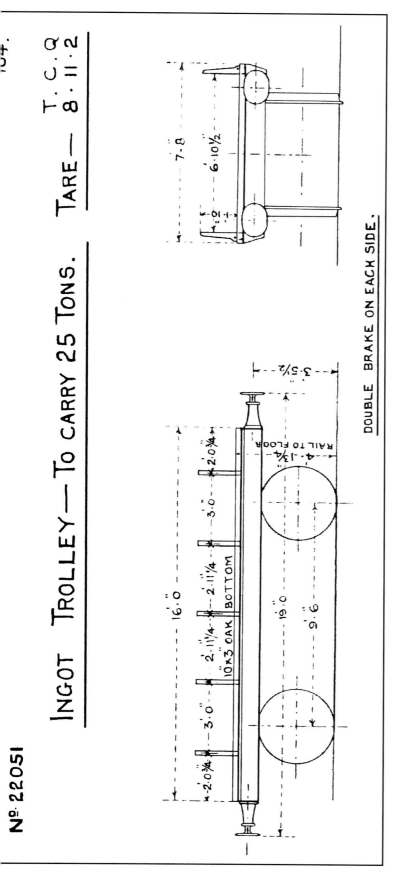

N⁰ 22051

INGOT TROLLEY—TO CARRY 25 TONS.

TARE — 8.11.2

T. C. Q

DOUBLE BRAKE ON EACH SIDE.

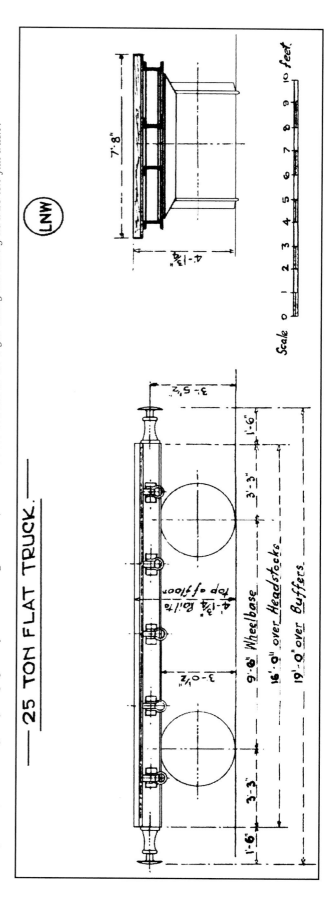

(LNW)

— 25 TON FLAT TRUCK. —

Scale 0 1 2 3 4 5 6 7 8 9 10 feet.

Figure 16, above: *Diagram 104 25 ton ingot trolley from the 1903 Diagram Book. According to notes on the diagram, it was fitted with two sets of binding chains with screw couplings, but the official photograph taken at Earlestown when it was new shows chains fitted to each of the five shackles along the side of the solebar.*

Figure 17, below: *Diagram from page 37 of the LMS Diagram Book, where it is descrbed not as an 'ingot' trolley but merely as a 25 ton 'flat truck'.*

Trolley to carry 20 tons Diagram 105

In 1911 six 'trolleys to carry 20 tons', as they are described in the *1903 Diagram Book*, were built as replacements for withdrawn Diagram 69, 15 ton boiler trolleys [*LNWR Wagons Volume Two*, page 145], as another step in the trolley up-grading programme, but they are perhaps better described as 'four-wheeled 20 ton well trolleys'.

They took the numbers of the vehicles they replaced: 18854, 18855, 28964, 28965, 28966, and 28967. Three more vehicles were built, one in 1912, which from the order in which the numbers are added to the original six in the *Diagram Book*, was No. 18853, one in 1915, No. 18856, both formerly Diagram 69, and one in 1917, No. 18860, formerly Diagram 74.

The diagram shows that the trolley was 27ft long over headstocks and 8ft wide. The well was 18ft 6in long with a central opening 11ft 3½in long by 2ft. The underside of the bed was 9in clear of the rails and the vehicle would pass round a curve of 2 chains radius.

A general arrangement drawing, Earlestown No. 840 dated 18th July 1910, survives as Historical Model Railway Society 1069 and shows much more detail. The body was built from riveted steel plate and angle sections. The central opening was 11ft 4½in long by 2ft, slightly larger than shown on the diagram. The 10-spoke wheels were 3ft 1½in in diameter and ran on 11in by 6in journals in oil-filled axle boxes. A screw brake was fitted to the right-hand end of each side and the coupling was the usual three-link style. The buffers and draw gear were operated by a single transverse leaf spring at each end and the buffers were fitted with oval heads. The bed of the well consisted of eight longitudinal rolled channel sections, fastened together by transverse brackets. It was largely an open structure, but the LMS diagram shows the section between the two outermost girders on each side to be filled by a wooden floor with four shackles per side recessed into the wooden planking. The wooden infill was probably an original feature, but the addition of the shackles was, almost certainly, a later LMS modification. At each corner of the bed was a chain box for the storage of the securing chains when not in use.

Two photographs of these wagons at work provide details of the LMS livery. For the LNWR livery the official photograph of the similar Diagram 106 chemical pan trolley, which was built in the same year, provides the best information available. For some reason, the *LMS Diagram Book* shows the length of the well reduced by one inch to 18ft 5in as it does for several other ex-LNWR trolleys.

All nine members of the class passed to the LMS in 1923 and continued in the service for the next twenty-five years. They are shown on page 96 of the *LMS Diagram Book*, where the only additional note is to the effect that the 'Assent of the Southern Railway is required before loading to the South Western section'. They all passed to BR in 1948 and continued in revenue service until the mid-1950s. One copy of the *LMS Diagram Book* records the demise of M228967 but gives no date and marks the other eight as sent to 'Service Stock in Scotland'. The subsequent withdrawal of most of them has been traced in the 1948-57 BR withdrawal registers. M228967 was withdrawn in 1952; 228966 in 1954; 228964 and 218855 in 1955; 218854 and 228965 in 1956; but there is no record of the withdrawal of the other three in this register nor in the more detailed 1958-67 register.

One survived into 'preservation' at the Kent & East Sussex Railway.

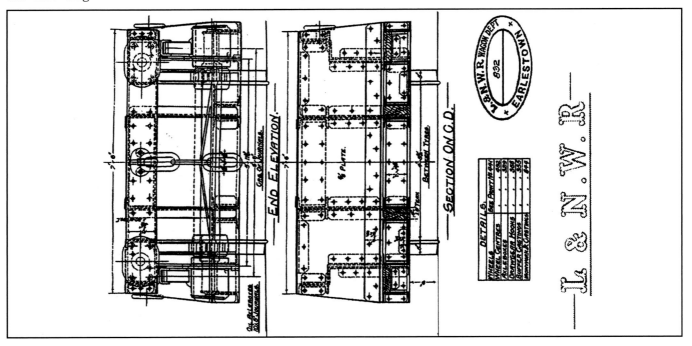

Figure 18: *End elevation and section from original drawing of Diagram 105 20 ton boiler trolley.*

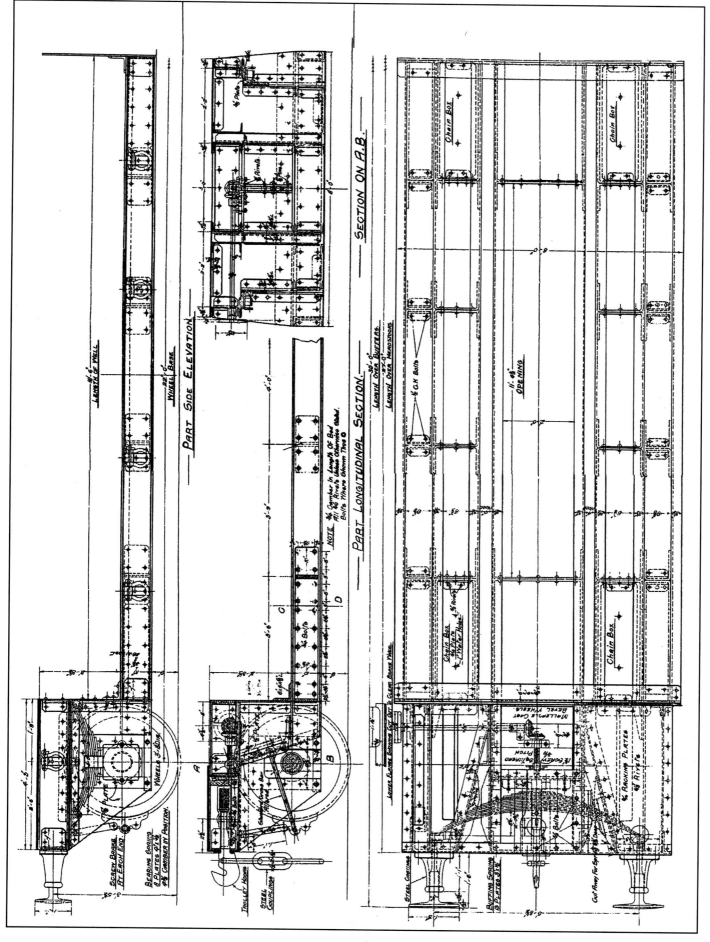

Figure 19: *Original drawing of Diagram 105 20 ton boiler trolley.*

21

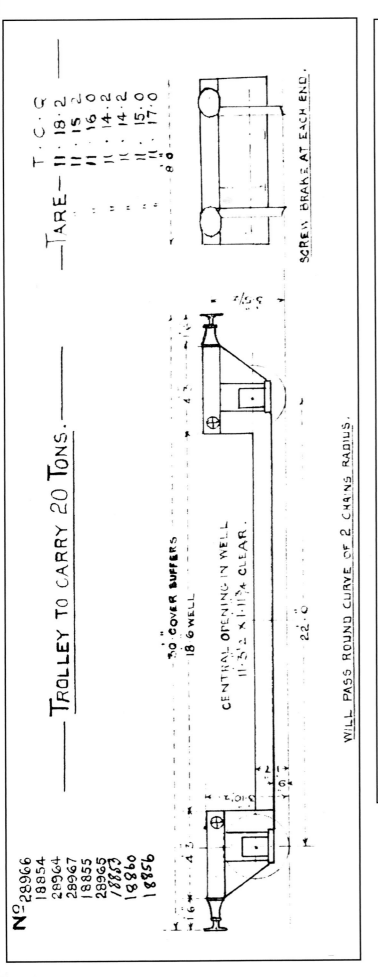

No 28966
18854
28964
28967
18855
28965
18853
18860
18856

TARE — T . C . Q
11 . 18 . 2
11 . 15 . 2
11 . 16 . 0
11 . 14 . 2
11 . 14 . 2
11 . 15 . 0
11 . 17 . 0

— TROLLEY TO CARRY 20 TONS. —

SCREW BRAKE AT EACH END.

30 COVER BUFFERS

18 6 WELL

CENTRAL OPENING IN WELL
11.3½ x 1.11¾ CLEAR.

22.0

WILL PASS ROUND CURVE OF 2 CHAINS RADIUS.

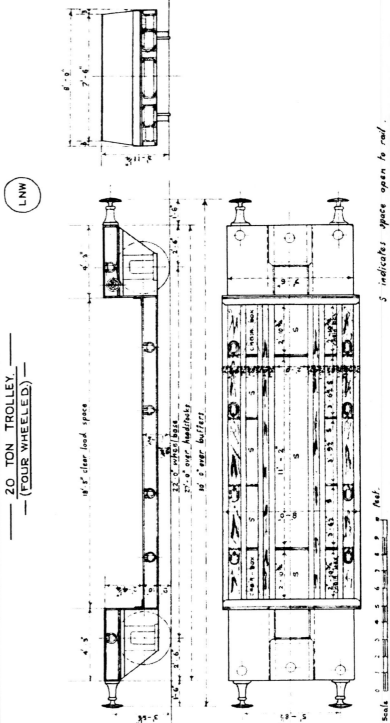

LNW

— 20 TON TROLLEY. —
— (FOUR WHEELED.) —

18' 5" clear load space

22' 0" wheelbase

25' 6" over headstocks

30' 0" over buffers

S indicates space open to rail.

Scale 0 1 2 3 4 5 6 7 8 9 feet.

Figure 20, above:
Diagram 105 boiler trolley taken from the 1903 Diagram Book.

Figure 21, right:
Diagram from page 96 of the LMS Diagram Book, where it is described not as a boiler trolley but merely as a 20 ton 'trolley'.

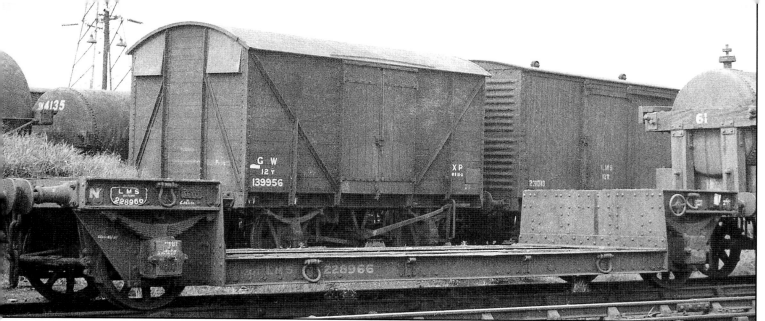

Plate 5, above: *LNWR No. 28966 in LMS livery as LMS No. 228966. In addition to the cast number plate, the number is painted on the left end of the solebar. On the channel section just under the left-hand platform is an 'N' to signify non-common user and a cast plate 'TYO', the LMS code for this type of wagon. The hand wheel for the right end brake and the LMS label clip are visible just under the right-hand platform.*

Plate 6, below: *No. 18855 in LMS livery in 1924. The livery is the same as in the above picture, but because this wagon is in new condition the tare weight, '11t. 17c. 1q.', is clearly visible at the right of the solebar on the original print. The hand-powered yard crane seems to be having no difficulty in loading or unloading the large diameter cylindrical vessel.*

Real Photographs E1174

Chemical Pan Trolley
to carry 12 tons
Diagram 61

The Diagram 61 chemical pan trolley was introduced in 1883. What exactly 'chemical pans' or 'caustic pots', as they were also described, were, and how they were loaded and unloaded, is uncertain, but they were used to transport caustic soda in the chemical industry in the Widnes area. Only the diagram of the design survives and shows it to be a rather crude, heavily constructed, vehicle with a single pair of wheels at each end and similar frame to the Diagram 69 boiler trolley and indeed to the Diagram 82 boiler trolley, which although they had eight wheels rather than four, have a similar body construction. No doubt the design was well suited to carry 12 tons in the heavy industrial environment for which it was intended.

The *LNWR Wagon Stock Age Book* for November 1902 records the dates when all six of these Diagram 61 chemical pan trolleys were built and one copy of the *1894 Diagram Book* is also annotated with the details. The first, 49200, was built on Capital account in 1883 at a cost of £118 16s. The second, 49995, was built on capital account in 1884 at a cost of £106 19s 11d. The third, 44779, was built on renewal account in 1887 by which time the price had risen to £132, while the fourth, 51829 built in 1890, on capital account, cost £128 19s 6d. The fourth had been sanctioned in Goods Conference Minute 15524, dated 1889, in the following terms: 'Recommended that another specially constructed vehicle be supplied to Widnes for the conveyance of caustic pots from that place'. Goods Conference minute 18414 dated 16th May 1898 sanctioned the building of two further chemical pan trolleys, numbered 66111 and 66112 in 1898.

The 1894 diagram is annotated that they all had no brakes but were fitted with binding chains to secure the caustic pots. It seems likely that they travelled from works to works in a special movement rather than on long distance goods trains. There is evidence that they had a hard life in that 49200 and 44779 had to be 'lifted', at an unknown date, to restore their rail clearance, as the springs had sagged under load.

The diagram records that the tare weight was 10 tons 3 cwt 3qr, and copies of the *1903 Diagram Book* have notes that 49200, 66111 and 66112 were fitted with a screw brake at one end, and the comment that 'these vehicles will pass round a curve of radius two chains'.

In 1911 Nos. 49995 and 51829 were withdrawn and renewed as Diagram 106 15 ton chemical pan trolleys. No. 66111 was given similar treatment in 1915.

Two of these rather crude Diagram 61 wagons were sufficiently serviceable to appear on page 85 of the *LMS Diagram Book*. The LMS diagram of 244779 and 249200 shows the rail clearance increased to 9¾in and the unrestricted length of the well reduced from 12ft to 11ft 4in. The two floor plans show details of the girders structure and openings. No. 266112 is not in the *LMS Diagram Book* and must have been scrapped early in the LMS era as its number was re-used for an LMS four-wheeled trolley built at Derby in 1928 (*LMS Wagons, Volume Two*, Essery, page 51).

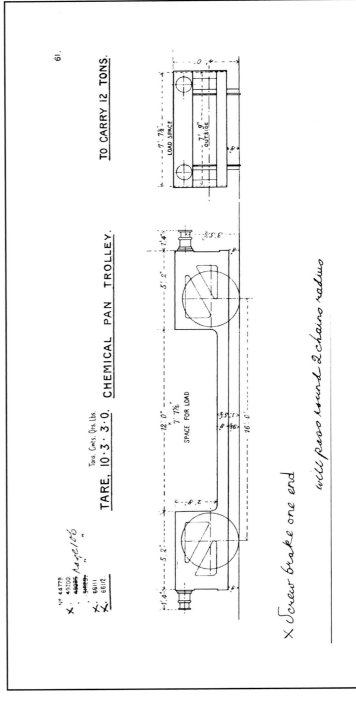

Figure 22: *Diagram of the 1883 design from the 1903 Wagon Diagram Book. Most copies have notes that vehicles marked with a cross had a single brake at one end only and that all would traverse a 2-chain radius.*

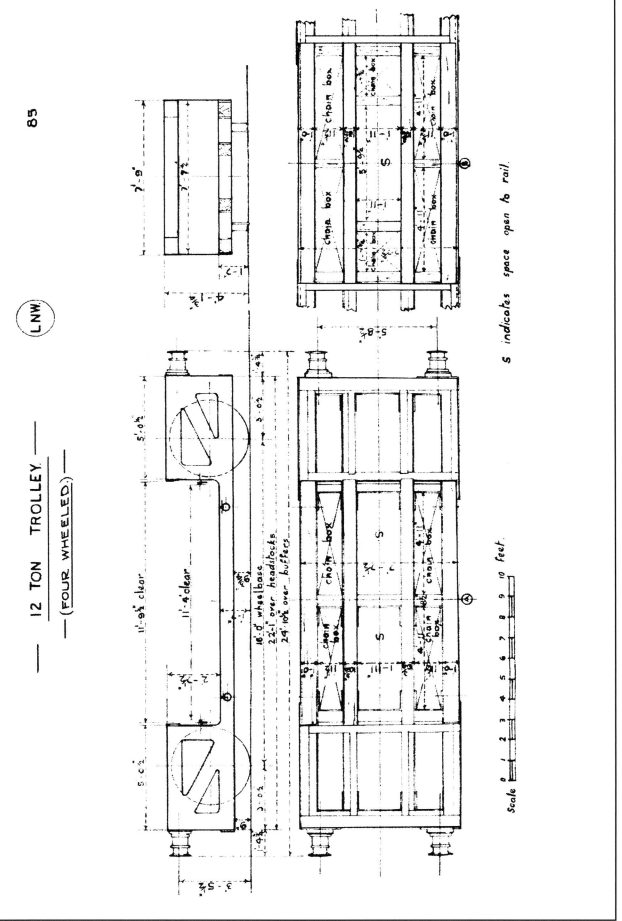

Figure 23: *Diagrams of two ex-LNWR chemical pan trolleys from page 85 of the LMS Diagram Book, showing the floor plan - plan 'A' refers to 244779 and plan 'B' to 249200 - and the layout of the chain boxes.*

Chemical Pan Trolley
to carry 15 tons
Diagram 106

This is a very different design from Diagram 61 and shows a more modern solution to the design of a chemical pan trolley. Earlestown general arrangement drawing 832 (HMRS 1516), dated 23rd September 1910, shows a vehicle that appears to be a shorter version of the Diagram 105 trolley, which was designed and built about the same time. Two vehicles of the new design, Diagram 106, were built in 1911 to replace two of the Diagram 61 chemical pan trolleys which were scrapped. The capacity was increased to 15 tons.

The general arrangement drawing reveals that these vehicles were built from steel sections and plate riveted together. The deck of the well was constructed as an open lattice of rolled channel sections, 9in by 3½in by 3½in, bolted and riveted together to form a strong platform to support the 15 ton load. There was a central opening in the floor to accommodate a downward projection of the load.

Shackles were bolted along the sides for the attachment of binding chains, which were stored, when not in use, in pockets at each corner below floor level. The underside of the well floor had only a 9in clearance above rail level, thus maximising the height of the load that could be carried within the loading gauge. The end sections, largely constructed from ⁵/₈in plate, housed the suspension system which consisted of 3ft 1½in wheels running in 10in by 5in journals supported on oil filled axle-boxes and bearing springs with seven plates measuring 4in by ⁵/₈in. Hand wheels were fitted at the right-hand end on either side of the wagon, to operate the brakes at that end, a single cast-iron brake block being fitted to each wheel. The buffers and draw gear were actuated by a single transverse leaf spring at each end and oval buffer heads were fitted from new. The trolley would pass round a curve of 1½ chains radius. In the official photograph of No. 51829 in new condition in May 1911, the tare weight is 9 tons 18cwt 2qr compared with 10 tons 4cwt recorded in the *Diagram Book* for the other vehicle of this diagram, No. 49995.

All three trolleys passed to the LMS in 1923 where they must have provided useful service, for they lasted long enough to enter BR ownership in 1948. The first to be withdrawn was 249995 in 1951, followed by 266111 in 1954, and the type became extinct when 251829 went to the scrap-yard in 1955.

Plate 7: *This rather fine official photograph provides a clear view of the overall appearance and livery of a Diagram 106 trolley when new in 1911. The same livery can also be assumed to have been used on the longer Diagram 105 trolleys built at the same time. The mode of consruction can be inferred from the pattern of rivet heads. Each group can be related to the flanges and cross-members forming the box structure of the vehicle.*

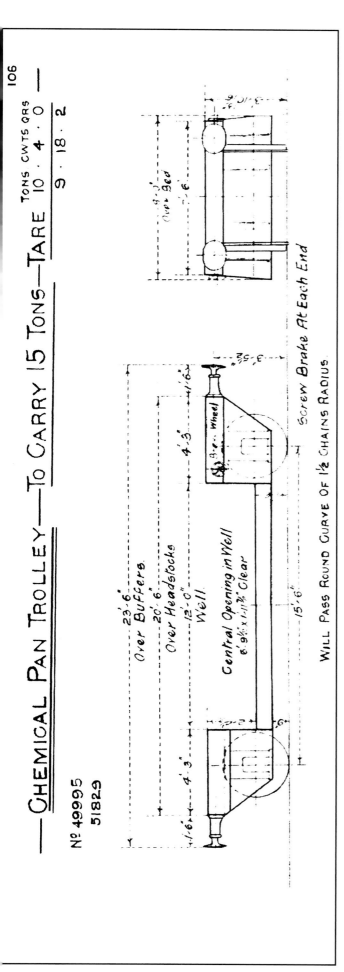

CHEMICAL PAN TROLLEY — TO CARRY 15 TONS — TARE
TONS CWTS QRS
10 · 4 · 0
9 · 18 · 2

Nº 49995
51829

Over Buffers.
23'·6"
Over Headstocks
20'·6"
Well
12'·0"

Central Opening in Well
6'·9½" x 1'·11¾" Clear

15'·6"

Over Sea

SCREW BRAKE AT EACH END

WILL PASS ROUND CURVE OF 1½ CHAINS RADIUS.

Figure 24, above: *LNWR Diagram 106 15 ton chemical pan trolley.*

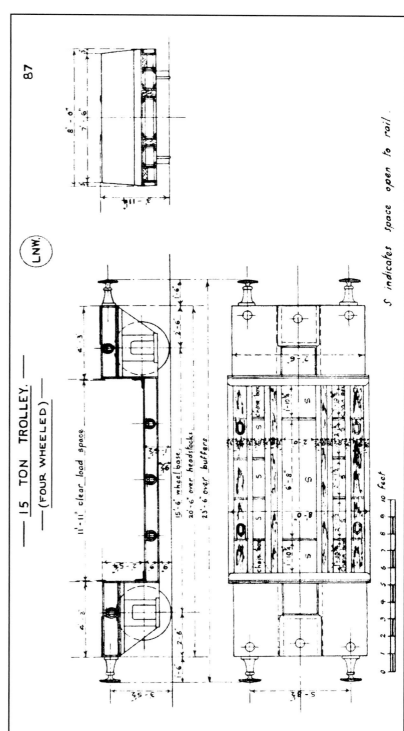

— 15 TON TROLLEY. —
— (FOUR WHEELED) —

LNW.

11'·11" clear load space

15'·6" wheel base.
20'·6" over headstocks
23'·6" over buffers

S indicates space open to rail.

0 1 2 3 4 5 6 7 8 9 10 feet

Figure 25, right: *Diagram of the 15 ton 'trolley' from page 87 of the LMS Diagram Book. The plan views are an interesting comparison with the LNWR diagram and give details of the floor of the well and the location of the open centre section. The length of the well has been reduced by one inch to 18ft 5in in a similar way to the bogie well trolleys to Diagram 101 and Diagram 102. This provided some ease to allow loads to be accommodated within the well.*

27

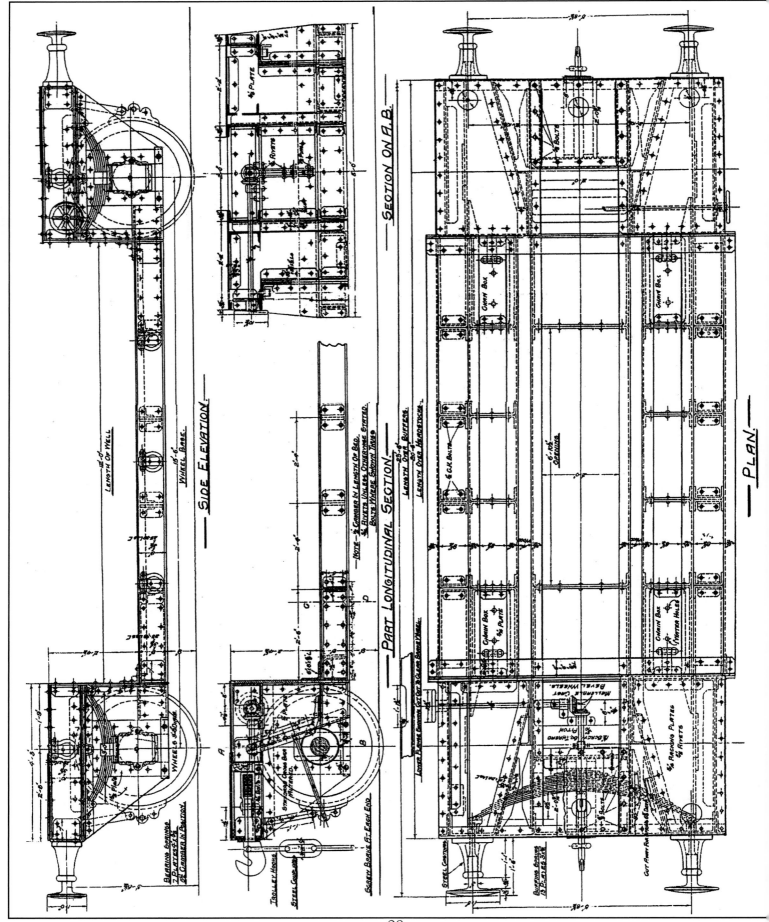

SIDE ELEVATION.

SECTION ON A.B.

PART LONGITUDINAL SECTION.

PLAN.

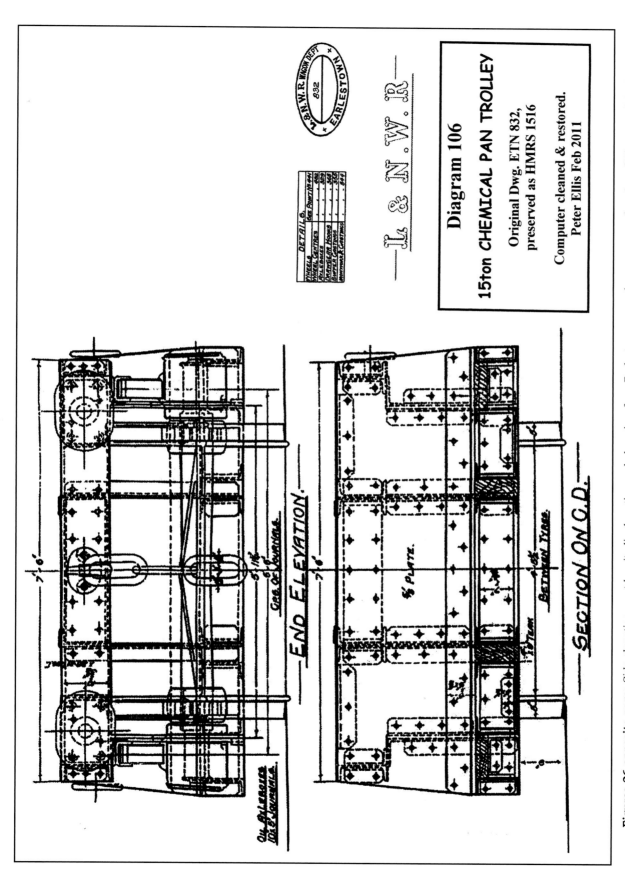

Figuree 26, opposite page: *Side elevation, part longitudinal section and plan view from Earlestown general arrangement drawing of Diagram 106 15 ton chemical pan trolley.*

Figure 27, above: *End elevation and section views.* ETN 832, HMRS 1516

Plate 8: *A former LNWR Diagram 103 18ft open single-plank wagon converted as a shunting/runner wagon still in service at Bletchley shed on 4th March 1959, where it seems to be acting as a runner wagon for the crane on the right. The running number is DM 18041. There is an LMS D-shaped number plate on the sole bar and the usual two small round cast-iron plates on the curb rail added by the LMS to its pre-grouping wagons. One gives the latest repaired date, the other reads: 'Built/Earlestown/191x LMS'. The wagon is fitted with double brakes on both sides, LMS flat-fronted oil-filled axle boxes, full length running boards and handrails, through vacuum pipes, twin-ribbed LNWR buffer castings and screw couplings. The headstocks have been replaced with the LMS standard square-ended type. The faded lettering at the right hand end of the single side plank includes the word 'BLETCHLEY'.*

Geoff Williams, courtesy Mike Williams

Plate 9: *General view of Bedford (St Johns) goods yard on 4th April 1914, showing a range of the more common LNWR wagon types but none of the special vehicles described in this book. The row on the left against the building starts with a Diagram 33 covered van followed by a Diagram 44 hopper wagon full of coal and a Diagram 17A goods brake van. Next in line is a Diagram 9 4-plank open wagon, two more Diagram 33 covered vans and finally two of the Diagram 88 18ft long covered vans introduced only in 1908. The middle rows consist mainly of 4-plank open wagons which cannot be positively identified at this distance. The row on the right starts with a 4-plank open wagon, followed by what appears to be a Diagram 103 18ft long single-plank wagon and two more 4-plank opens. Next in line is a Diagram 33 covered van and two of the larger Diagram 88 vans - there is a noticeable difference in height between these vehicles. It is just possible to identify a 4-plank open and another Diagram 88 van, but beyond that point iden-tification becomes very difficult, although at the end of this line there is a cattle wagon identifiable by the whitewash on its lower planks. The wagon loads of cinders on the right nearest the camera perhaps come from Bedford's small engine shed which closed eventually in 1924.*

Courtesy David J. Patrick